THE 10 DEADLIEST ANIMALS

BY RACHEL ROSE

Minneapolis, Minnesota

Credits

Cover and title page, © Graham Prentice/Alamy Stock Photo, © Ken Griffiths/Shutterstock, and © Steve Bloom Images/Alamy Stock Photo; Title Page, © Graham Prentice/Alamy Stock Photo; 4, © Yü Lan/Adobe Stock Photos; 5, © Ivan Kuzmin/Alamy Stock Photo; 6–7, © Panther Media GmbH/Alamy Stock Photo; 8, © AkimaFutura/Adobe Stock Photos; 8–9, © Ken Griffiths/Adobe Stock Photos; 10–11, © Sergey Uryadnikov/Shutterstock; 11, © Andrew Holt/Getty Images; 12–13, © Gary Bell/ Oceanwide/ Minden Pictures; 14, © gudkovandrey/Adobe Stock Photos; 15, © Wayne Marinovich/iStock; 16–17, © Ralph Lee Hopkins/Alamy Stock Photo; 17, © Jamesbowyer/iStock; 18, © Ondrej Prosicky/iStock; 19, © Ken Griffiths/Getty Images; 20–21, © panom/iStock; 21, © I love nature/Getty Images; 22T, © donvanstaden/Adobe Stock Photos; 22M, © Juan Gärtner/Adobe Stock Photos; 22B, © AndyDiamond/iStock; 23, © Ken Griffiths/Alamy Stock Photo.

Bearport Publishing Company Product Development Team

Publisher: Jen Jenson; Director of Product Development: Spencer Brinker; Managing Editor: Allison Juda; Editor: Cole Nelson; Associate Editor: Naomi Reich; Associate Editor: Tiana Tran; Art Director: Colin O'Dea; Designer: Kim Jones; Designer: Kayla Eggert; Product Development Specialist: Owen Hamlin

Statement on Usage of Generative Artificial Intelligence

Bearport Publishing remains committed to publishing high-quality nonfiction books. Therefore, we restrict the use of generative AI to ensure accuracy of all text and visual components pertaining to a book's subject. See BearportPublishing.com for details.

Library of Congress Cataloging-in-Publication Data is available at www.loc.gov or upon request from the publisher.

ISBN: 979-8-89232-639-1 (hardcover)
ISBN: 979-8-89232-688-9 (ebook)

Copyright © 2025 Bearport Publishing Company. All rights reserved. No part of this publication may be reproduced in whole or in part, stored in any retrieval system, or transmitted in any form or by any means, electronic, mechanical, photocopying, recording, or otherwise, without written permission from the publisher.

For more information, write to Bearport Publishing, 5357 Penn Avenue South, Minneapolis, MN 55419.

CONTENTS

Dangerous and Deadly 4

#10 Deathstalker Scorpion 5

#9 Golden Poison Dart Frog 6

#8 Sydney Funnel-Web Spider 8

#7 Great White Shark 10

#6 Australian Box Jellyfish 12

#5 Lion 14

#4 Hippopotamus 15

#3 Saltwater Crocodile 16

#2 Inland Taipan 18

#1 Mosquito 20

Even More Deadly Animals 22

Glossary 23

Index 24

Read More 24

Learn More Online 24

About the Author 24

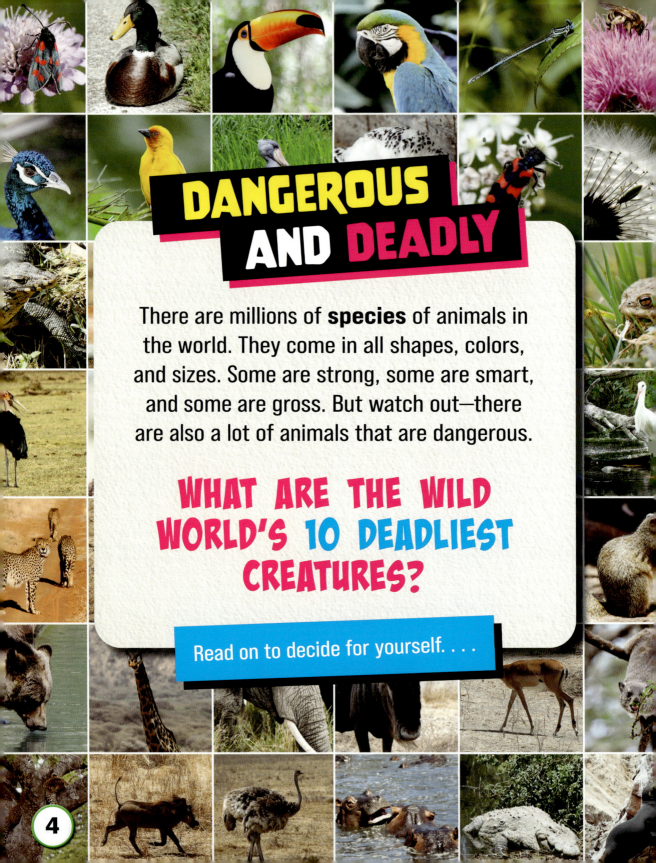

DANGEROUS AND DEADLY

There are millions of **species** of animals in the world. They come in all shapes, colors, and sizes. Some are strong, some are smart, and some are gross. But watch out—there are also a lot of animals that are dangerous.

WHAT ARE THE WILD WORLD'S 10 DEADLIEST CREATURES?

Read on to decide for yourself. . . .

#10 DEATHSTALKER SCORPION

Watch where you step! One sting from a tiny deathstalker scorpion could kill. With a name like deathstalker, it's no wonder this is one of the deadliest species of scorpions. It strikes a deathblow with a **venomous** stinger at the end of its tail.

Scorpions have been around for millions of years—since before dinosaurs existed.

Deathstalkers hunt mostly small insects and spiders.

A deathstalker's pale color helps it blend in with its dusty, sandy desert **habitat**.

5

#9 GOLDEN POISON DART FROG

They may look small and cute, but don't be fooled. Golden poison dart frogs are some of the most dangerous animals around. Just one touch could be deadly. These frogs ooze poison from the **pores** on their skin. A single golden poison dart frog has enough poison to kill up to 20,000 mice—or 10 adult humans!

How do these frogs become poisonous? Scientists think the deadly stuff comes from the food they eat.

Golden poison dart frogs live in the rainforest.

#8 SYDNEY FUNNEL-WEB SPIDER

Want to play hide-and-seek? A Sydney funnel-web spider combines venom with tricky hunting tactics for lethal results. The sneaky spider doesn't stalk prey. Instead, it builds trip lines across the entrance of its web and then hides until prey passes by. Once an animal crosses the silky trip line, the spider jumps out of hiding to take a deadly bite.

Funnel-web spiders spin their webs into tunnel-like funnels.

#7 GREAT WHITE SHARK

What's that huge shadow in the water? It's a great white shark! These big fish can grow up to 21 feet (6.4 m) long and weigh up to 5,000 pounds (2,300 kg). That's bigger than an SUV! White sharks have about 300 jagged teeth. They use the sharp chompers to rip apart prey. Stay away from this fierce fish!

Great whites have up to seven rows of razor-sharp teeth.

These huge sharks can sniff out prey from miles away.

#6 AUSTRALIAN BOX JELLYFISH

Why might an underwater animal earn the nickname sea wasp? Australian box jellyfish have millions of stinging cells on each of their 60 **tentacles**. The cells use mini needles to deliver venom to any unfortunate prey. *Ouch!* And unlike other jellyfish that just float, these jellies are able to swim to chase down their next meal. Watch out!

More than 100 people die every year from box jellyfish stings.

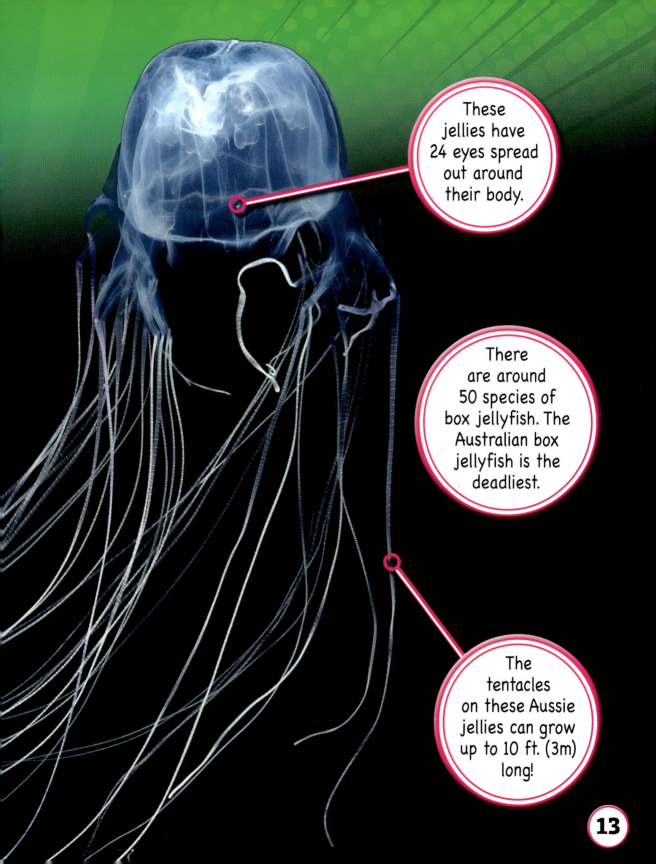

#5 LION

Lions are often called the king of beasts. These powerful animals are the only big cats that live and hunt in groups. They chase down their prey, running up to 50 mph (80 kph) to catch their victims. Then, they surround the poor animal, going in for the kill as one.

A lion's roar can be heard up to 5 miles (8 km) away.

Female lions do most of a pride's deadly hunting.

A group of lions is called a pride.

#4 HIPPOPOTAMUS

Beware some of the most deadly animals in Africa—hippopotamuses. Known to be very **territorial**, hippos will fight to the death to defend their families and homes. Their big **tusks** and huge size make them very dangerous when they attack. The big beasts will go after other hippos and sometimes even people!

Hippos kill between 500 and 3,000 people every year.

The powerful jaws of a hippo can split a boat in two.

Male hippos can be as heavy as a grand piano.

#3 SALTWATER CROCODILE

There are hungry mouths under the water. Saltwater crocodiles hunt almost anything, from little frogs and fish to big buffalo and wild boar. They hide underwater while waiting for their prey to get near. Then, they burst out in a surprise attack. The crocs chomp down on their prey, pull their victims underwater, and spin around. This rips larger prey into pieces. It's dinnertime!

Saltwater crocodiles have the strongest bite force of any animal on Earth.

The crocodile's fatal underwater spin is known as the death roll.

Stay back from this croc's mouthful of 66 teeth, which it uses to grip its prey.

More than 1,000 people are killed every year by saltwater crocodiles.

#2 INLAND TAIPAN

Would you want to meet the world's most venomous snake? Just one bite from the inland taipan contains enough venom to kill about 100 people! Luckily for humans, the slithering snakes prefer to hunt **rodents**. Inland taipans are extremely fast and vicious when they attack. The snakes usually strike their prey many times. A rodent meal doesn't stand a chance.

The inland taipan is also called the fierce snake.

#1 MOSQUITO

The deadliest animal is so small you may never see it coming! While most mosquitoes are harmless, a few species are responsible for more than one million human deaths each year. These tiny insects can quickly spread deadly **diseases**, such as malaria and yellow fever. A five-second bite can turn fatal if one of these diseases takes hold.

A mosquito can suck up to three times its weight in blood.

Almost half of the world's population lives in areas with malaria-carrying mosquitoes.

Scientists aren't sure why, but mosquitoes bite more often during full moons.

Only female mosquitoes bite humans. They need the blood to make eggs.

EVEN MORE DEADLY ANIMALS

These 10 animals aren't the only ones to fear. What else should you stay away from?

ELEPHANT

An elephant's massive size can make it deadly. You wouldn't want to end up underfoot with an elephant running by.

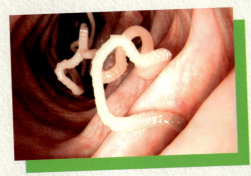

TAPEWORM

Though relatively small, tapeworms are terrifying. They make their homes in the digestive systems of other living creatures and eat their victims from the inside out.

HYENA

When it comes to hyenas, their bite might be just as bad as their bark. These social animals hunt in deadly packs.

GLOSSARY

diseases illnesses or sicknesses

habitat a place in nature where an animal or plant normally lives

pores tiny holes in an animal's skin

rodents small mammals with long front teeth, such as rats and mice

species groups that animals are divided into, according to similar characteristics

tentacles long, thin limbs that hang down from a jellyfish's body

territorial having a strong desire to defend an area against intruders

toxic harmful or deadly

tusks long, pointed teeth, such as those on a hippopotamus or an elephant

venomous full of poison that is released through a sting or bite

Index

bite 8, 16, 18–22
death roll 16
diseases 20
habitat 5
humans 6, 18, 20–21
insects 5, 9, 20
poison 6–7
prey 8–12, 14, 16–18
species 4–5, 13, 20
sting 5, 12
teeth 10–11, 17
tentacles 12–13
tusks 15
venom 5, 8–9, 12, 18–19
webs 8

Read More

Ganeri, Anita. *Deadly Mammals (Deadly Creatures).* New York: Rosen Publishing Group, 2022.

Hofer, Charles C. *Cuddly but Deadly Animals (Killer Nature).* North Mankato, MN: Capstone Press, 2022.

Learn More Online

1. Go to **FactSurfer.com** or scan the QR code below.
2. Enter "**10 Deadliest Animals**" into the search box.
3. Click on the cover of this book to see a list of websites.

About the Author

Rachel Rose writes books for kids and teaches yoga. Her favorite animal for all time is her dog, Sandy.